Me, Myself, and MS

GWENDOLYN POWELL

authorHOUSE®

AuthorHouse™
1663 Liberty Drive
Bloomington, IN 47403
www.authorhouse.com
Phone: 1 (800) 839-8640

Published by AuthorHouse 08/08/2017

ISBN: 978-1-5462-0294-3 (sc)
ISBN: 978-1-5462-0293-6 (e)

Library of Congress Control Number: 2017911996

This book is dedicated to my husband of forty years,

our children and grandchildren, my mom and dad,

and all those who have loved, laughed, and gone on

this journey with me. And to my neurologist,

Dr. Susan Calkins.

Terms and phrases you will encounter throughout this book:

MS (multiple sclerosis)
My little monster
Steroids
Now the fun begins

Chapter 1

Okay, say you wake up one morning and your right hand is numb. That's how my journey with multiple sclerosis (MS) began. I thank God that I had and still have a wonderful husband and that our children were fourteen and sixteen years old. I was only thirty-five when what I call "my little monster" crept into my life. I always prayed to God to let me stay around and be healthy enough, at least until my children were old enough to take care of themselves. I am now fifty-eight, my children are thirty-nine and thirty-seven, and we have six beautiful grandchildren.

My journey began in March 1994, when my numb hand turned into a numb arm and I was stricken with double vision. I went to see my primary care doctor, who examined me and told me there was no medical reason for the numbness in my hand and arm. I politely told the doctor that although she might have a medical degree, I had lived in this body for thirty-five years and I knew something was seriously wrong.

I quickly found a new doctor, who sent me for a nerve study test to see if I had carpel tunnel syndrome. When the technician saw me holding on to my husband for support, she asked what was wrong. I told her I had double vision and was seeing two of her. She quickly called in the neurologist on duty and they did the nerve study test, which revealed what I already knew: no carpel tunnel. After examining me, the neurologist told my husband and me that I had a serious neurological problem.

At that point, the fun began. I had my first MRI scan. My double vision made me extremely dizzy and the room seemed to be spinning, but they wanted me to lie still on my back in this machine that looked like a tunnel for at least forty-five minutes. Before the test, my doctor gave me a motion sickness patch to see if it would help with the dizziness, but the patch did nothing. My world just kept spinning.

My husband and I during my dizzy spell.

This part of my story is for black women, or women with hair texture similar to ours. My hair was permed, but it hadn't been touched up or combed in about five weeks. Yes, my husband had bathed me every day, but I had spent all that time in bed. I hadn't wanted to move at all, let alone have someone messing with my hair. So when I went for my test, I wore a hat. I thought no one would see my hair, so I didn't care what it looked like. Since that was my first MRI, I didn't know that I couldn't have anything on my head. When the MRI technician asked me to remove my hat, my husband and I laughed for the first time in weeks. The lumps and bumps under that hat were worse than the double vision, and that's all I'm going to say. I lay on the MRI table, dizzy from what I now know was an MS symptom and embarrassed because of my hair. After I felt a whole lot better, I went to my beautician. She thought my hair had broken off because I had done nothing to it all those weeks. But after she permed it, it grew about two inches.

About five minutes into my MRI, I flipped out. I started screaming and trying to get out of the machine. They pulled me out and my husband calmed me down. But when they started again, the same thing happened. My husband had to hold one of my legs to keep me calm, so that they could complete the test. It took two or three hours to complete a test that should have lasted only forty-five minutes.

About five years before the numbness in my hand and arm, I had temporarily gone blind in my left eye. At that time, I had been told that my migraines had shut off a blood vessel, which caused the blindness. The vessel had eventually reopened, and I had regained my sight.

Now the MRI test revealed no brain lesions, so our next step was a spinal tap. At that point, I didn't care—I just needed to know what was wrong with me. Okay, the spinal tap was no picnic. In fact, it felt like a herd of elephants was sitting on the lower half of my body. Afterward, I had to lie on my back without moving for about three hours, but I had no headache or other side effects.

The results came back in about a week, and my doctor called to set up an appointment so that we could talk in his office. Later that day, my husband drove me to my doctor's office, but of course there were no parking spaces in front. I told him that I could make it inside the building, where I would wait for him. I had a patch over one eye for the double vision, so instead of seeing four people out of two eyes, I was seeing two people out of one eye. Cross your eyes and then uncross them, and you'll see what I'm talking about.

As I got out of the car, I was dizzy and weak. (Who can eat when it feels like you're on one of those rides that just goes around and around?) Inside the building I sat down close to the door, in what I thought was an empty chair. Then I heard a voice behind me say, "Excuse me, miss. Are you all right? You're sitting on my lap." The kind woman gently moved me to an empty chair and waited with me until my husband arrived. She even asked if someone could get me a wheelchair.

We proceeded upstairs to the doctor's office to get my test results. As he tried to explain my problem, all I heard was "fluid" and "brain stem." The tears started, as my mind went in all different directions. At first I thought he meant I had a brain tumor. It took my husband, the doctor, and his nurse to calm me down. Then I heard "multiple sclerosis." I wondered, *What did he just say? And what is multiple sclerosis?* The spinal tap showed protein in my spinal fluid, a sign of MS. As my doctor explained, MS is treatable, but I had to take my health in my own hands and learn more about what I was facing.

The first course of treatment was steroids to help with the inflammation. We tried steroids by mouth for a week or two, but when that didn't work, I started IV steroids. After unsuccessfully trying dosages of 250, 500, and 750 mg, the magic number turned out to be 1,000 mg. My vision returned to normal after five days at 1,000 mg, but the pain in my eyes, an unexpected side effect, lasted for a couple of weeks.

I wasn't told in advance about the possible side effects from the steroids, which included nightmares, muscle spasms from the loss of potassium, little to no sleep, acne, and what is called a *moon face*. I have a long, narrow face, and the steroids made me look like I was hoarding food in my cheeks. I resembled a teenager with a severe case of acne on my face *and* my scalp. And finally, I developed a temper and started snapping at everyone.

Chapter 2

When I was diagnosed with MS, I was working full time, taking college courses two days a week, and raising two teenagers. My husband was on disability after back surgery, so I was helping him out as much as I could. Anyone who has had back surgery knows what pain he was going through.

It took me six to eight weeks to recover from my first MS attack. (I call it an attack because it feels like your body is being attacked and you have no control over it.) With my sight back and the dizziness gone, my husband and I went to the library to do our research on MS. There is so much to learn—what medications work for what symptoms, what to do and not do, medical terms, medical equipment if needed, and so on. For example, I learned that heat is not your friend if you have MS. We also joined our local chapter of the National Multiple Sclerosis Society.

No parents want to hear that their child has an illness, no matter how old the child is. When I told my parents that I had MS, my dad took it as well as could be expected. My mom, however, said the doctor was wrong and walked away from me. When we told our son, who was fourteen, he accepted the news. After all, he was young and had no clue about MS except what we explained to him. The news hit his sixteen-year-old sister harder. She is now thirty-nine and remains somewhat quiet about the fact that her mom has this illness. As a family, we all had a hard time trying to wrap our minds around what we were facing. My husband I decided to let our children come to terms with it and deal with it on their own.

We went to our first MS meeting as a family, minus our daughter.

When I asked my mom to go with us, she said, "For what? There is nothing wrong with you." It really hit home when I saw people using walkers, wheelchairs, and canes. MS does not discriminate—young and old, all ethnicities. We began by sharing our name and the year we got our diagnosis. Then we were asked by the counselor to share our stories about MS and its effect on us and our families. I was frightened by the despair and "Why me?" from some people.

We were asked to imagine going down a long path, not knowing what awaited us at the end. It was like a horror movie—no sunshine, loss of mobility and sight, loneliness. Generally my husband and I can find smiles and laughter in almost any situation, even by just looking at each other. He slowly took us down a dark, rainy path overhung with bare tree limbs, and at the end was some sort of monster. Everyone looked as though they were in shock. But when he and I looked at each other and started laughing, we could hear our laughter slowly spread across the room. He had let everyone know how scary they had just made their own life stories, and as a result, the mood in the room lightened considerably.

We attend all of our remaining sessions. By that time my mom had come around a little and started asking what we talked about at meetings. Then she surprised me and asked if she could come along, so she attended the last two sessions. At our last session, it was time to say goodbye and the tears started. We had come to know and care about each other, and we shared a common bond. We exchanged phone numbers and addresses so that we could keep in touch with an occasional phone call or letter to see how everyone and their families were doing.

I was then on Betaseron, one of the first approved drugs for MS, which I took every other day. I experienced some side effects including fever, chills, headache, pain and redness at the injection site, and muscle spasms. The side effects would last about twenty-four hours, and just as I started to feel better, it was time for another injection.

Chapter 3

After three months I was able to return to work, although it took a little adjustment. My employer was great, and I fully disclosed my illness. During one of our MS meetings, some people had said they felt ashamed and embarrassed, as if they had something to hide. I felt none of that, however, because MS can strike anyone at any moment. I neither wanted nor needed any special treatment or accommodations.

I started having attacks every three to four months, with symptoms including numbness, weakness, and optic neuritis. My feet would go from cold to hot in a matter of minutes, and my leg dragged on occasion. Some attacks required IV steroid treatments, since steroids by mouth still didn't work for me. I would take off work six to eight weeks at a time, sometimes returning only to have another attack and go out for another six to eight weeks. Sometimes I would work half days for a few weeks until I was strong enough to work a full eight-hour day.

I love walking, stationary bike riding, and any type of aerobics, so I would exercise five or six days a week, either before or after work. My daughter, who still wanted no part of MS, would exercise with me. That's how we spent time together, but whenever I was sick, she would stay in her room or at a friend's house.

I went to work on May 12, 1995, from 6:00 a.m. to 2:00 p.m. Then I got off work, cooked dinner, rode my stationary bike, and went for a walk with my daughter around her high school track. We returned home and ate dinner, and I watched TV until around 12:30 a.m. I am sure you are wondering how I remember these events so well.

This is why. On the morning of Saturday, May 13, 1995, at around five o'clock, I felt like the life was going out of the left side of my body. It started in my face, which I could feel starting to droop. Then I felt heaviness and tingling in my left arm and hand, which moved down my leg and into my foot. By then, the left side of my body was paralyzed. I tried unsuccessfully to sit up and started to panic. I tried to call my husband's name, but the words were so slurred and slow that he did not respond. I hit at him with my right hand, and he awoke to see the left side of my face drooping. I was so scared that I started crying.

Remaining cool, my husband called 911 and our HMO. (Choice words were spoken between my husband and our HMO operator, who was taking this as a joke.) Meanwhile he was trying to calm me down. I told him that I needed to use the bathroom and that he needed to wash my face, brush my teeth, and get me dressed before the paramedics came. How he understood what I was saying is a mystery to me. I guess after being together for so long, we can read each other's minds—even when the words make no sense. He carried me to the bathroom and back to our bedroom, and then dressed me. Granted, I ended up wearing my T-shirt and stretch pants backward, but I was dressed.

By this time the paramedics had arrived. My husband explained to the 911 dispatcher what my symptoms were and that I had MS. The dispatcher said it sounded like a stroke, but my husband was sure that I was having an MS attack. In front of our home were two ambulances and a fire department hook-and-ladder truck, which, as we found out later, carried lifesaving equipment. I was still crying, and the sight of eight paramedics standing in our bedroom did not help. They thought that I had a stroke because there was no movement on my left side and my face was drooping, but my husband explained that I have MS. They took my vital signs and tried to find a vein to start an IV drip, but they were unable to do so. I have these tiny veins that roll as soon as you hit them, so the paramedics just had to rush me to the hospital ASAP.

The staircase leading to our bedroom is narrow, so the paramedics had to carry me—still crying—down the fourteen steps on one of their makeshifts beds. Our son was home and had to witness all of this, but our daughter—thank God—was sleeping over at a friend's house. My husband asked his brother, who lived around the corner from us, to come and get our son so that he could go to the hospital with me.

My husband managed to beat the ambulance, sirens and all, to the hospital, which is only about seven minutes away. During the drive, the paramedic talked and sang to me to try to calm me down. The first face I saw, when the doors on the ambulance opened at the hospital, was my husband's. They quickly got me settled into the emergency room and started an IV. Still crying, I lost control of my bladder in the hospital bed. It takes a special type of caregiver to deal with someone who is sick and afraid. The nurse changed my wet clothes, dried my tears, gave me a big hug, and said, "Baby, you are going to be all right."

My husband called my mom from the emergency room to let her know what had happened. She wanted to hear my voice, but all she got on the other end of the phone were my sobs. The ER doctors did a CAT scan to rule out a stroke. Then the attending doctor called my neurologist, who wanted me transferred to another hospital. Transport arrived at about eleven o'clock that morning. The other hospital is forty minutes away, and yes, I was still crying. Again my husband managed to beat the ambulance to the hospital, and when the ambulance doors opened, the first face I saw was his. By the time I got to my hospital room, my tears had finally stopped. I was all cried out, and it was around one o'clock in the afternoon.

My family members started to arrive—mom and dad, son, sisters, brothers- and sisters-in-law. Everyone except my daughter, who was not ready to deal with what had happened to me. My mom touched my left side from my face to my feet and asked if I could move my fingers. Reality had not yet set in for her. I give her a crooked smile, to tell her that I was all right, and she smiled back. Then my family gradually left, one by one. My husband wanted to stay all night, but I was right across from the nurses' station, so he knew I would be well cared for.

When my neurologist showed up, the first thing she said was "If you want me to continue to be your doctor, I want you to retire. The stress of your job and the long commute are contributing to your frequent attacks." I agreed, and she examined me. She ordered my 1,000 mg IV steroids, other medications, and pureed foods, and then she put me on strict bed orders. I was not one to just lie around, so I asked if I could have one of those bedside toilets so that I would not have to use a bedpan. She agreed, but I had to call a nurse to get me on and off the toilet. She put in the order and all was okay, or so I thought.

I had to use the bathroom in the middle of the night—two thirty or three o'clock—so I buzzed for the nurse. No response. I buzzed again. Still no response. With the toilet right beside my bed, I figured that I could use my right side to pull myself up and would be able to sit on the toilet. Boy, was I wrong. I held on to the bedrail and pulled myself up. Okay, that went well. Sitting on the bed, I used my right hand to pull my panties down. So far, so good. But then why did I try to stand up on my own? Luckily for me, the draw curtains that divided the room were there. With my panties around my ankles, I lost my balance, grabbed the curtains, and slowly slid down the curtains, back and forth, until I finally hit the floor. The drop to the floor wasn't too bad, since I was holding on to the curtains for dear life.

Lying facedown on the floor, I could see the nurses' station. Not a nurse in sight, but I figured someone would see me lying there on the floor and help me. Meanwhile my roommate, who was in a coma-like state, heard nothing. After resting facedown on the floor for a while, I got myself together, pulled myself back up those same curtains to the side of the bed, and was finally able to lie back down. A few minutes later, the nurse arrived to check on me and take my vital signs. She took my pressure and said, "Mrs. Powell, your pressure is a little high." All I could say was "Yes, and can you please help me onto the toilet?" That was the first and last time I tried to get up by myself. One thing I can say for certain, though, is that those are some strong hospital curtains.

The next morning my husband arrived around seven thirty, kissed me, and asked how my night was. When I told him about my on-the-floor nightmare, he said, "Sweetie, you need a shower. You smell like fear and urine. I didn't want to tell you yesterday, since you had been through so much." He had brought all my soaps, lotions, and powders with him that morning. He asked the nurses for a shower chair and bathed me. I smelled like a newborn baby when I got back in my hospital bed.

My daughter came to see me the next night with her friends. I heard her crying as she came up the hall to my room, where she fell across my stomach and cried like a baby. There was no calming her down, so I asked her friends to please take her home. I told her that I was all right and that I loved her.

It was Mother's Day. Happy Mother's Day to me. I spent the next eight days in the hospital, with my mom standing guard over me. She would answer the phone in a whisper, "She's asleep. May I ask who's calling?" My husband was there from morning to night. Coworkers were in and out, though my supervisor told them to limit their calls and visits. "She needs her rest," she said, and I did. My dad popped in during his breaks at works. Company is nice, but when you are so fatigued and drained, rest and sleep are welcomed guests.

Physical therapy two or three times a day was demanding. I was still paralyzed on my left side, but my doctor agreed to let me go home with strict conditions. I was so excited to be going home that I could not drink the breakfast that I had ordered that morning. My husband arrived early to take me home, and we were waiting for the discharge papers. The nurse noticed my untouched breakfast and asked, "You didn't eat this morning?"

Without thinking, my husband replied, "No, I was not hungry." We had to laugh when he realized the nurse was talking to me, the patient.

My tears started again when we got to our front door. My husband asked what was the matter, and I told him that I was just glad to be back home. My doctor had ordered a hospital bed so that I could stay on the ground floor, but it wouldn't arrive until the next day. So I slept on the couch that first night, with our children and the dog on the floor next to the couch. My husband was the only family member with enough sense to sleep in a bed.

I don't know why pit bulls have been labeled as dangerous dogs. My dog, Spice, was a loving and protective pit bull. When the hospital bed arrived, she pulled her dog bed from our son's room, where she usually slept, to the foot of my hospital bed in the living room. Every time I moved, she would come to the side of my bed to see if I was okay. When I was able to get around using a cane, she would even walk beside me to the bathroom and wait outside the door for me. She would not lie back down on her bed until I was settled in my bed. My husband slept in a recliner in the living room with me.

My Dog Spice

Chapter 4

I had to go to physical therapy thrice weekly, for two- to three-hour sessions, to gain back strength on my left side. We turned those therapy sessions into a family trip with my mom and dad. What a sight. I was using a cane, and my husband was also on a cane because of his back. One day, on the elevator at the hospital, people were starting to stare. One woman finally asked if we had been in a terrible car accident. We replied "No," looked at each other, smiled, reached our floor, and told everyone to have a nice day. As the elevator doors closed behind us, they all had puzzled looks on their faces.

Since I had lost the use of my left arm and hand, my hand had balled up into a tight fist. My doctor wanted a half cast to be made so that my hand would not lock into that position. The therapist and her assistant tried to un-ball my hand, but it would ball right back up. The therapist's hand was the same size as mine, so we used her hand to make the mold for the cast. The fit was perfect.

Therapy was *hell*. After each session, I was worn out. I also had to do therapy at home seven days a week. The cast fit across the back of my hand and arm, with Velcro to hold it in place. Two or three times a day, my husband had to remove the cast to uncurl and massage my hand. Thank God I am right handed. My left arm and hand were still paralyzed, the left side of my face was still a little droopy, and my speech was still slurred. I could only creep along with the help of my cane, but at least I was walking.

My mom came over every day to cook and help out around the house, and to be with me. One day she became concerned that MS had started to affect my mind. We live in Maryland, and our mailbox is at the end of our driveway. If we need the mailperson to pick up some outgoing mail, we just raise the little flag on the side of the mailbox. One day I was sitting in my recliner, which my parents had bought for me so that I would be comfortable without having to stay in that hospital bed all day. My mom was in the kitchen cooking chili, and my children had just come home from school. I asked them how their day had been, and whether they had put the flag up for the mailman.

My mom, who lives in the District of Columbia, had no clue about the flag on the mailbox and what it meant. When she heard me ask the kids about the flag, she looked as if she wanted to cry. She kept coming from the kitchen into the living room where I was sitting, as if she wanted to ask me something. But then all she could do was stare at me and rub my hair. This went on for hours. Later that night when she got home, she got up enough nerve to ask me if I remembered talking about a flag being on my mailbox. She admitted that she was worried about me. All I could do was laugh. When I explained the flag on the mailbox to her, I could hear the relief in her voice. Every time she comes over to our house or we are traveling, and she sees a mailbox with a raised flag, this same story comes up. She was so glad that I was not losing my mind.

My last company affair was that year's Fourth of July picnic. I had already told my employer that I would be going out on disability. It was hard saying goodbye to my employer and coworkers for the last time, but I had new challenges and opportunities ahead of me.

By July, two months after I was paralyzed, I still had not regained use of my left arm and hand. I would focus and tell my mind that all I had to do was move one finger at a time and then move my arm off my lap. Needless to say, that didn't work, but I kept trying. Finally, after about eight weeks, movement started to return. One finger, two fingers, and then the whole hand.

When the nerves started to come back to life, however, the pain was severe. I have a high pain threshold, but that had me in tears. I was so glad that my children were at school that day, because I sat in my daughter's room on her bed and just cried. I was in so much pain.

I know that there are those who don't believe, but I looked out my daughter's window up into the sky and said, "Lord, I can't take this pain." I have never asked, "Why me? I am too young for this." I've never questioned my MS, but I could not deal with that pain. As soon as I admitted to God that I couldn't handle it, however, I felt the pain leaving. After that day, I regained control of my whole left side. My husband started to design a brace for me that would work like a hand, to help me pick things up and to serve as a hand, just in case I did not regain full use of my left arm and hand.

At the MS meetings, we learned about the MS walk, which raised awareness and funds for research and other outreach programs for people with MS. My son and I raised money and signed up for our first MS walk, which was in Virginia. We started at Pentagon City and ended up at Glen Echo Park, twelve miles away. After the first three or four miles, I told my son that I must have lost my mind. How was I going to make it another eight miles? As I was dragging myself along, we were passed by a lady walking by herself, with a limp and using a cane. She was my inspiration to go the distance.

We rested a little more than halfway to the finish. That was a mistake, because when we got up to continue, our legs were stiff and weak. With one mile left to go, in front of us was this hill. I looked at my son and said, "I am going to hold on to the back of your pants, and you are going to have to help pull me up this hill." As we went up the hill, his pants slowly started coming down. He had to hold up his pants along with his momma. We finished our twelve-mile walk in four and a half hours, and I wasn't even sore the next day.

By that time I was taking the second approved MS drug, Avonex.

We walked and raised money for the MS Society for several years. It started out with just me and my son, but it grew to include my husband and daughter, other family members, friends of family, friends of friends, and even coworkers. We went from just the two of us to a team of seventy-five or more. We put time and effort into naming our teams, and there are stories behind some of our team names. My husband named our first team Let's Strike a Blow Against MS, which was printed on the back of our T-shirts with a boxing gloves graphic.

After all, I had just started my fight with this illness. Jesse's Angels was in memory of my nephew who was killed in 1997. I came up with the name for our Family Ties T-shirt, which really hit home for me.

I even spelled out what MS meant to me:

Must
Undo
Lost
Time
In
People's
Lives
Every day

Someone
Cares
Leaving
Everyone
Racing
Onward
Securing
Immediate
Solutions

And yes, I came up with every word attached to the letters spelling out *multiple sclerosis*. My husband's quote at the bottom of our T-shirts was dedicated to me:

You are #1 above the rest,
and you completed a big test.
Your courage hefty and strong will
will help you climb up life's big hill.

I could not have fought this battle without my husband by my side. He has been there from day one, never complaining. Through my bad temper, my moon face, he has been someone for me to lean on, someone to wipe away my tears, always there morning and night to tell me that he loves me. I thank God each and every day for him. I am going to stray just for one moment to share a poem that he wrote to me:

My Breeze

Like a breeze through an open window she came
All over my soul, changing my spirit from brass to gold.
Who is this fine lady? This uninvited guest?
Whoever she is, I know that I am blessed.
Just like a fine rose, her smell does linger.
Her love I must have, must put the ring on her finger.
I married this breeze that I love so much.
Hope you all find your breeze as I found mine,
Coming into you from a window or a door.
One thing for certain, her love I do adore.
For my breeze, I will have forever more.

Back to our MS walks. The president of the MS Society in Washington, DC, had heard about me and wanted to meet me. She said that she loved my spirit and determination, and she asked if news channel four in Washington, DC, could interview me before the walk began. I did the interview and was asked questions like, "What inspires you to do these walks?" My reply was, "Look at all the support that I have. I am not in this alone. I'm here to bring awareness to this illness." I was interviewed two years in a row.

About a week before one of our walks, my right leg started to drag. That was the first time I had experienced an MS attack just before a walk. I told myself that I could make the twelve miles, even with a bad leg. Mind over matter. My team members noticed me dragging my leg from the parking lot to the check-in point. They all wanted to know if I was all right and whether I'd be able to make our three-hour walk. My husband and children knew that I was dealing with a bad leg at the time, but no one else knew. Of course, me being who I am, I told them that I was fine, that my leg muscles were too tight but the walk would help loosen them up.

By the third mile, however, my son and brother-in-law were on either side of me, holding on to my arms. My dad, who was in his sixties, walked with us every year. He was keeping a close eye on me and finally said, "Okay, Gwenie, that's enough. I don't think you should try and go any farther." I knew that I couldn't make it any farther, because I was almost being carried at that point. We sat for a while, and then my family hailed a cab for me and told me that they would see me at the finish line. My team walked the remaining nine miles, so they were my legs that day. Remember when I said that I cried only once because of MS? When I got into that cab, I cried for the second time. I felt like I had failed, and that MS had gained the upper hand. I was waiting at the finish line for my team members, who all arrived about two hours later. They clapped for me. Okay, so then I cried for the third time, only because I knew how proud they were of me for trying.

For our next walk, we were able to persuade our daughter to walk with us, even though she was still having a hard time dealing with my illness. My daughter was a glamour girl, so she wore dress pants and a button-down blouse with her tennis shoes. That was the first year that it rained, but we were prepared. We all had umbrellas and my mom had brought rain ponchos for everyone, but my glamour girl wouldn't put on her poncho. It didn't match her outfit, so she just put her jacket over her head. A portion of our walk was along the C & O Canal on a dirt path that had turned to mud because of the rain. Glamour Girl was pissed and fussing. The coat that was over her head was soaked—and did I mention that it was a little chilly that day? Her dress pants had mud all over them and she was dragging behind us. To make matters worse, her brother played like he was going to push her into the water. We laughed the whole twelve miles—everyone except Glamour Girl, that is.

That year it took us four and a half hours to finish. Bus service was provided to take everyone from the finish line back to the starting point. After we ate the lunch provided by the MS Society, we were waiting for the bus. My dad turned to Glamour Girl, his granddaughter, and said,

"How about we just walk the twelve miles back?" Laughter erupted. That was Glamour Girl's first and last walk.

My husband was finally able to join us one year because the route was wheelchair and scooter accessible. He had had a back operation, but he was able to use an electric scooter that our cousin had given to us. (To this day, I have never used or needed to use that scooter.) My husband charged the batteries overnight, and the next morning they put the scooter in the truck and off we went. Everyone thought that he was the one with MS, since he was using the scooter. People were asking him, "How long have you had MS?"

He would answer, "I'm fine. My wife is the one who has MS." I'm standing there with no cane, walker, or scooter, and looking healthy as ever.

Like I tell people, I might look healthy, but if you flip me inside out, you'll see the lesions on my brain and spine. What you see on the outside is different from what's on the inside. I get dirty looks from people when I park in a space for people with disabilities on days when I don't feel well. You never know what someone might be going through or dealing with. Appearances can be deceiving.

MS WALKS

Chapter 5

When I had my first optic neuritis attack, it felt like someone was stabbing me in my eye. Any light that hit my eye was painful, so I wore sunglasses in my house day and night. The curtains had to stay closed, and my husband even put blankets over them to keep out any extra light. I hoped that the pain and sensitivity to light would clear up on its own, but there was really no chance of that happening. So my friend, Mr. 1,000 mg IV steroid, had to step in to help the healing process along.

After five days, the pain was reduced and I was able to tolerate a little light. But the side effects from the steroids returned, and so the jokes began. Remember, our household has always been filled with laughter. "Hey, Mom, with all those steroids, can you lift our house and carry it to another neighborhood?" Ha ha ha, not that kind of steroids. When my steroid-induced bad attitude moved in, the jokes moved out. It had snowed eight or nine inches that winter, but I was so mean and snapping at everyone that my children were willing to walk four miles through the snow to my sister-in-law's house, just to get away. Even my pit bull kept her distance. My sight was back to normal in about eight weeks.

Those of us who have MS know what heat does to our bodies. I loved aerobics, especially step aerobics, but the sweating it causes and strength it takes left me looking for another form of exercise. My doctor suggested water aerobics, but there was no way I was going near any body of water except my shower. When I was a preteen, I had almost drowned at a beach. So I was afraid of three feet of water at the swimming pool, and I would hold on to the edge of the pool for dear life. My husband, being the sweet and supportive man that he is, spoke up and said, "Baby, I will teach you how to swim." Easier said than done.

My first swimming lesson with my husband went like this: "Okay, baby, trust me. I will not let anything happen to you." I trust my husband with my life. He finally eased me away from the edge of the pool and into about four feet of water. I'm only five feet tall, so you know my heart was racing and I was starting to panic. Somehow I found myself on my husband's back, screaming and fighting him. Good thing it was early afternoon and the pool was almost empty, because I did embarrass us just a little. Once my husband got me off his back, literally, and back on the pool deck, he said, "We'll pay someone to teach you how to swim."

When I signed up for swim lessons at our neighborhood pool, I had no idea how much fun it would be. My adult beginner lessons lasted for two months, three nights a week. At the first lesson, we met our instructor and introduced ourselves to each other. Then it was time to get into the pool. I was in three feet of water and clinging to the edge. Old habits are hard to break. Our first task was to put our heads underwater with our eyes open and then tell the instructor how many fingers he was holding up. And yes, he went under with each of his students. How did I know that? The only student still dry from the waist up, I had no clue how many fingers he was holding up—nor did I care. Three lessons later, I was still dry from the waist up and still had no clue whether he even had any fingers. Every night after I got home from my "swimming lessons," I would tell myself, "Tomorrow I will go underwater and count the instructor's fingers."

During lesson four, I finally got up enough nerve to go underwater and count the man's fingers. When I came up and out of the water, I shouted, "Two fingers! Two fingers!" The class broke out in applause. After that class, I gradually built up more confidence. I learned to float and, yes, even swim underwater. My classmates nicknamed me Flipper. To pass the class, we had to jump off the high dive wearing a life vest. The instructor was waiting for us in twelve feet of water. When it was my turn to jump, I looked down from the high dive and told my instructor to promise that he would not move until after I hit the water. I jumped, I went under, and I felt like Dora the Explorer—I did it, I did it! After I completed Adult One classes, I signed up for Adult Two swimming lessons, which started the very next night.

I was thirty-seven years old when I learned how to swim. My new workout turned out to be water aerobics after all. I have also taken deepwater aerobics. Never assume that you can't do something until you try—and then keep at it until you accomplish what you set out to do.

I love swimming. My husband and I went swimming in Jamaica at six o'clock in the morning. I was swimming on my back in sky-blue water. Looking up at the sky gave me a feeling of being carefree and knowing how wonderful life is, even with this illness.

Swimming in Jamaica

Learn to Swim

This certifies that

Gwendolyn Powell

has participated in a swimming class for

Primary Skills
Level II

Comments

You did well
in adult II.

Keep up the good
work in adult III

Next class to register for

Adult III

Learn to Swim

This certifies that

Gwendolyn Powell

has participated in a swimming class for

Water Exploration
Level I

Great job!
You'll do well
in Adult II !!

Next class to register for

Adult II

Swimming Certificates

Chapter 6

My mom and dad used to say that God has all the pieces to the puzzle, and I could see that my puzzle was just starting to come together.

Our first grandchild was born in 1998, when our son was only nineteen years old. He had just started his first year of college, and I was only thirty-nine. He was working, going to school, and raising his daughter. He wanted to finish college, so I told him that I would babysit since I was on disability and not working. At that time, my husband was also on disability because of his back surgery. That worked out nicely, because I could not have watched her by myself. My hands, feet, and legs had a mind of their own. I would pick up a cup and drop it, bump into things, and trip over nothing. So there was no way that I was going to drop or bump my "Sweetie Girl." Her smiles and giggles made me laugh on days when otherwise I would have just felt like crying.

Our son trusted me with his daughter because he knew that if she slipped out of my hands (Thank God, she never did!) or if I bumped her going through a doorway, it would be because my limbs had stopped communicating with my brain. One Saturday, my son and I took Sweetie Girl to Chuck E. Cheese. When we returned home, I lifted my grandbaby out of her car seat and … The next thing I knew, I was lying on top of her in our driveway. She was only about a year and a half old, but the look on her little face said, "Grandma, what just happened?"

Her dad was so calm. He helped me up first, since I was lying on top of his baby. Then he picked up his daughter and asked if we were all right. Somehow I had managed not to put all my weight on her when

I fell. My grandbaby did not cry during or after our little spill. Like my mom and dad used to say, God protects fools and babies, and my precious little grandbaby sure needed protecting that day.

Our daughter got married and moved to Jamaica in 1997. She and her husband were expecting their first child, our second grandbaby, in September 1999. I wanted to give her a baby shower, so she came home when she was about four month pregnant. My sister-in-law Jan, her son Chris, and I went shopping for food and other party goodies for the baby shower. When I have a lot on my mind, I tend to say out loud whatever I'm thinking. We had finished shopping and were at the checkout counter, when I looked at the cashier ringing up my groceries and asked, "Paper or plastic?" Of course, he should have asked *me* that question, so he was quite confused. My sister-in-law and I just laughed, because she knows all about me and my illness.

But her son, my nephew, had a sad look on his face. He was young at the time and found no humor in some of the changes that he was beginning to see in me. He had studied and learned as much as he could about MS. He volunteered at the MS walks and participated in the MS readathon, and when he was old enough, he joined in the MS walks with me. He is older now, but he still has trouble finding humor in my illness. Trust me, there is lots of humor in coping with MS. You have to laugh— and laugh a lot. If you don't, you'll find yourself crying and singing the "Why me?" song. I have had MS for twenty-three years now, and I have never sung the "Why me?" song. But I have laughed until I cried, because of some of the things I have been through with MS. I have no time for a pity party. It's time to laugh, live, and move on to the next phase of my life.

Our daughter had given birth to our second grandchild, a baby boy, so we went to Jamaica to meet our grandson. When my daughter asked me if I wanted to bathe him, I wanted to say yes, but I knew that a tiny baby, soapy water, and a baby bathtub on top of the dining room table was not a good combination. Afraid of letting my grandson slip out of my hands, but with a big smile on my face, I undressed him and started to bathe him. I was praying the whole time, "Lord, please don't let my grandson and his tub hit the floor." Thankfully, we made it through the bath and a feeding before he fell asleep in my arms.

While in Jamaica, I wanted to do all the things that I had seen on those TV commercials. My husband, son, and niece were with me, but I was the only one with heat restrictions and a problem with fatigue. So I planned our adventures and sightseeing for early mornings, before the real heat moved in. Our first adventure was water rafting, which wasn't physically taxing at all—just relaxing.

Water Rafting and Chilling on Bench in Jamaica

Bathing my Grandson

Next we went horseback riding, for only the second time in my life. Here's how my first experience with horseback riding had gone. I had put one foot in the stirrup, thrown my other leg over the horse, and fallen off the other side. The attendant or horse patrol person—let's just call him the man in charge of the horses—helped me up and told me that a horse, like a car, has a gas pedal and a brake pedal. To make your horse go, you kick him with both feet. To make your horse stop, you pull his reins. Simple, right? Well, I was kicking and pulling the reins at the same time, so the poor horse was confused. Does she want me to go or stop? Finally the horse had turned around and tried to bite me. When he raised up on his hind legs and rocked me from side to side, I had grabbed him around the neck and held on for dear life. I had told my husband and son to go ahead, and that I would catch up with them once I got the hang of horseback riding.

When the horse tried to throw me, I screamed my husband's name. Our son, riding with his father in the woods, heard me and asked, "Isn't that Mom calling you?" Then a group of riders passed me and my horse. My horse was what you call a follower, so when he saw the group riding past us, he took off and chased them. I wrapped my arms around his neck, hollering for help, while he played catch-up with his friends. One woman—let's call her my angel—circled back, took my horse by his reins, and led us back to the stables. I thanked her, while panting as hard as my horse. When the stable attendant again tried to explain how to control the horse, I said, "You can keep the money that I paid for the hour-long ride. Just get me the hell off this horse."

So now we were in Jamaica for my second try at this horseback riding thing, and they brought out their biggest horse for me. I got up on one side—and almost immediately went back down the other side, but our tour guide caught me. At first I was so scared that our guide had to lead his horse and mine, but gradually I became comfortable and began riding all by myself. I had a ball! We even rode down to the beach and into the water. Riding a horse through the water is difficult, because it's hard to keep your feet in the stirrups. The pressure of the water tries to turn them backward. I even had a little gallop going on when we were back on land. It started to rain toward the end of our horse tour and we got soaked, but we had so much fun.

HorseBack Riding

Then we went parasailing. They hooked us up to what looked like a big kite, took us out on a boat, and launched us five hundred feet into the air. What a great feeling! It was so beautiful up there—just a calm, relaxed feeling of freedom. I closed my eyes for a few moments, felt the wind against my face, and just let my mind and body go. If you are ever on an island, try it and you'll understand.

Parasailing in Jamaica

Our last adventure was to climb Dunn's River Falls, which was difficult and called for a group effort. Our tour guide told us that holding hands would help us face the challenge of height, rushing water, and slippery rocks. As we headed up the falls, we saw a man holding on to the fence and bleeding from his legs, but I just looked at him and kept going. I was climbing between my son and Sharneice, my niece. If I was going down, they were going with me. But when my son started falling, I let go of his hand real fast. They were going down with me—I was *not* going down with them, because I could not have taken a fall like that. When my son came up out of the water, he had lost one of his swimming shoes. We even fell backward into a part of the falls that was like a little pond. Finally, we made it to the top of the falls. Mission accomplished.

Climbing Dunn's River Falls

The only things that I didn't get to do were snorkel and ride a Jet Ski, but I'll do those on my next trip. I've always said that if something looks like fun, I'm going to try it—as long as I'm able-bodied and God gives me the strength.

Finally our trip came to an end and it was time to say goodbye to Abbey, our grandson. Sweetie Girl, who was just a year and four days older than her cousin, had pointed at him and tried to say *baby*. But the word had come out as *abbey*, so that name stuck with him. Sweetie Girl had also named her *granddaddy*, when that word came out as *gaggy*. So Abbey and Sweetie Girl's grandfather now goes by Gaggy.

When we left Jamaica, our daughter would not look at me. I kissed her and told her I loved her. I held my grandson and kissed him until his little cheeks were moist. I had to hold my tears back and be strong for my daughter, but as soon as I got to our hotel room, I cried like a baby. My daughter called me when they got home and told me that she had cried all the way home. We have a very close relationship. My daughter, son-in-law, and four beautiful grandbabies still live in Jamaica. We call each other three or four times a day, seven days a week. The distance between us has not changed a thing.

Last day in Jamaica

Our daughter visited us every three months with Abbey, or we would go to Jamaica and see them. On one of their trips home, I was talking on the cordless phone when I walked by Abbey and his mom. As I reached out to rub his little cheek, the phone slipped out of my hand and hit him on top of his head. He was only three months old, and I felt so bad. His mom was a little upset, Abbey being her first baby, but that's how first-time moms are. She got over it, and I managed not to drop him or bump him into anything else. Two grandbabies, two minor accidents—not bad at all.

My mom used to worry about me doing too much. She would say things like, "You need to rest and take it easy." But my dad was cool, because he knew that I was not going to keep still unless I really felt bad. He enjoyed hearing about my daredevil adventures and what I was planning to do next. I scared my mom once, when it took me two months to bounce back from a bout of optic neuritis. She came over to our house to help out, and I wasn't doing any smiling or laughing. So when I felt a little better, I had my husband take me over to my parents' house. I have a key, so I didn't let them know that I was coming over. I just popped into the kitchen where my parents were eating dinner, and you should have seen the smile on my mom's face. She said, "I'm so glad to see you and that you are back to your normal self again." She now tells everyone that I won't stand still for long and that I'm too strong willed to let MS keep me down. I told my mom that when I'm not going and going, and when my laughter stops, that's the time for her to worry about me. I have always told my family and friends that I might have MS, but MS does not have me. I refuse to give in or give up.

Chapter 7

While I'm on the subject of trips, this next story has to do with me tripping and almost falling flat on my face. One year, my older sister was having a Labor Day cookout. I'm known for my potato salad, so I went shopping with my son and Sweetie Girl to buy all the makings. I sometimes had trouble walking up my driveway anyway, but when flip-flops got added to the mix, that was a really bad combination. Shoes like flip-flops and slip-ons don't mix well with MS.

It was a cool evening, so I was wearing a jacket with my cell phone in the pocket. Out of the car I stepped, with a grocery bag containing glass jars of dill relish in one hand. Somehow the top of one of my flip-flops rolled underneath my foot. The next thing I knew, I was staggering forward out of control—and then stretched out on the sidewalk. My cell phone was lying halfway down the driveway, and the batteries were in the grass. My son came to my rescue. He helped me up and asked, "Mom, are you okay?" Then he retrieved my phone and put it back together, much like he keeps having to do with me. I had scraped my toes, knees, and knuckles, but I somehow managed to keep the jars of dill relish from hitting the ground. Don't ask me how. That must have looked pretty funny, like I was diving for a baseball in center field. Those striped flip-flops now belong to my daughter.

My husband and I used to take trips to Atlantic City with my mom and dad. Dad especially enjoyed those trips; in fact, he would go at least twice a month by himself. Atlantic City was my little getaway from my MS treatments. At that time I was taking Betaseron by injection every other day. I had some of the typical side effects, such as flu-like

42

symptoms, so the beach, boardwalk, and slot machines helped to take my mind off how I was feeling. I was also developing red spots wherever my husband gave me my Betaseron injections, so I looked like some strange red leopard. My mom and I would walk the boardwalk early in the morning and after the sun went down. My husband came up with the idea of me carrying an umbrella, so I had my own personal shade wherever I went.

MOM and DAD

No new MS symptoms or funny stories on our trips, except that one evening I was amazed to see my dad eat an entire fried chicken by himself. I didn't eat dinner that night, because if I became overheated, I would lose my appetite and other unfortunate things would happen. Okay, I'll just say it—uncontrolled bowels. (I didn't want to leave you wondering.) My mom had never forgotten the flag on the mailbox incident. So on our trips up and back from Atlantic City, she would start laughing and ask me if I remembered that time she had thought I was going crazy. Yeah, I'm the crazy one and she's the one still laughing.

The one time my doctor got really nervous was when I had an attack of transverse myelitis. First my feet went numb for a couple of days. I hoped it would just go away, but the numbness spread to my knees and then to the top of my thighs. Remember how you felt, as a little child, when you played outside in the snow too long? Remember how your hands and feet would get so cold that they hurt? That's how the lower half of my body felt. I couldn't stand for anything to touch my legs—no pants or socks. Even the sheets on our bed felt like someone was scratching me with needles. Finally admitting that things were not getting better, I called my neurologist. The numbness had spread to the top of my breasts and down both arms to my hands. I had even started to lose my voice, and I was hoarse when I spoke with my doctor.

She told me to come to her office as soon as possible. Putting on clothes was horrible, because I was numb from the top of my breasts to the tip of my toes. Needless to say, my doctor was upset with me for having waited so long to contact her about such a serious attack. The first thing she did was ask me to swallow a little cup of water. I didn't choke, but if I had, she would have sent me straight to the hospital. Choking would have indicated that the numbness was spreading to my throat, which could have caused me to stop breathing. Then I would have been put on a ventilator. She wanted to admit me anyway, but I did not want to go.

Despite my hoarse voice, she trusted me to go home under one condition. She knew that my husband wasn't working at the time and that he would be home with me twenty-four seven. She told him that if I choked, even once, he was to take me to the closest emergency room. Of course, she started me on my 1,000 mg IV steroid treatments for five days. You know you have a good doctor when she calls you— morning, noon, and night, including weekends—just to see if she can detect a change in your voice. If my voice had gotten deeper, she would have admitted me into the hospital. After my steroid treatments, the numbness left my body and my voice returned in about five weeks. It felt good to sleep under the covers with my husband, instead of him under the covers and me on top.

In 2001, our third grandbaby was born—a baby girl. We call her Dedda Momma. The whole process—going to the hospital, staying with my daughter through thirteen hours of labor, and spending some time with them afterward—kept me up for almost twenty-four hours, which took a toll on my body. Confusion starts to set in when I'm up for a long time like that. My daughter wanted to have a natural childbirth, but eventually she started begging for something to relieve the pain. All parents try to be strong for their children, but certain things can make you break down. My daughter had her whole coaching team there with her—myself, her cousin, and her aunt Cathy. During her final phase of labor, she looked up at me from her hospital bed and said, "Mommy, it hurts so bad that I'm going to cry."

I've called her Big Girl since she was born, and I told her, "Please don't cry, Big Girl. Because if you cry, I'll start crying too." Sure enough, she looked at me and busted out crying.

From there, it was all downhill. I started crying, which made her cousin cry, and then even the nurse started to cry. Aunt Cathy, a social worker, was the only one who maintained her composure. She looked at us and said, "This is pitiful. The whole coaching team has fallen apart." When she informed us that she was going out in the hallway to find a new coaching team, our tears turned into laughter. About ten minutes later, my granddaughter was born.

It normally takes about twenty-five minutes to get home from the hospital, but that night it took me two hours. Because I was so tired, my sense of direction was gone and I was all turned around. I drove under the same bridge, going in circles, over and over again. Every time I got to one particular stoplight, I would tell myself to turn, but then I'd head for that same underpass again. Finally I called home, admitted that I was lost, and asked for help. I felt like I was in that movie *Groundhog Day*. My son gave me directions over the phone, turn for turn, until I finally got home. The moral of this story is that if you need to stay up for twenty-four hours, take a couple of catnaps.

Between the births of my three grandbabies, I had mild MS flare-ups. But I got plenty of rest, so I didn't have to take any steroids.

MS has a way of keeping your mind and mouth from working together. You might be thinking one thing, but out of your mouth comes something quite different. One day when my son and I were in downtown Washington, DC, I asked him about the new "guide tours." He looked at me and started to laugh, and right away I knew that I had said something wrong. He said, "Mom, you meant to say *tour guides*." I have turned so many words around backward—*tus boken* (bus token), *bite butter* (butt biter), and so on. I tend to switch the first letters and create my own words, but my family usually understands what I'm saying.

One day I told Jan, my sister-in-law, that I wash my face outside of the sink. (Sorry, but it would take me too long to fully explain this one.) We laughed on the phone for a couple of minutes, and Jan knew what I was talking about. You have to laugh your way through this illness. Otherwise you'll spend half of your day crying and the other half worrying about how you'll feel tomorrow. I thank God for my gift of laughter and my positive attitude and outlook on life.

After my daughter moved to Jamaica, my son and I would spend Saturdays together. He worked for the YMCA, and he persuaded me to join the gym they had opened about eight minutes from our home. We took classes at eight and nine o'clock in the morning. Sometimes I would walk on a treadmill or do some light weightlifting, depending on how I felt. We spent two and a half to three hours at the gym on Saturdays. Exercising still gives me energy and keeps me pain-free without muscle cramps.

At checkups with my neurologist, she would tell me to keep exercising my muscles, since it obviously worked for me. She has been my neurologist since I first got my diagnosis of MS. She knows that I know my body and what is happening with it regarding MS. If I call her for an appointment, she knows that I am not doing well.

After the gym, my son and I would go shopping. He would ask what I wanted—shoes, pocketbook, earrings, whatever—and if I wanted something, he'd buy it for me. We would have a nice lunch or dinner, depending on what time it was. Some Saturdays we would not get home until eight or nine o'clock at night. One Saturday we were gone from eight in the morning until nine o'clock that night. I had asked him that day what time it was, and he said eleven minutes after seven, but it sounded to me like he said three o'clock in the morning. We had been gone all day, so it seemed like three o'clock in the morning to me.

You know the saying, "Daddy's girl and Momma's boy"? Well, we have one of each. My dad used to say to my son, "You are always with your mother," just playing with him. He'd tell my son that he was a momma's boy, and my son would reply, "I sure am." He would watch me closely while we were at the gym to make sure that I was all right. Some Saturdays I would be moving slowly, so he would walk on the treadmill right beside me and keep an eye on me. Now he is thirty –seven years old and we still spend some Saturdays together. My husband and I always tell our children how proud we are of them and what good parents they are to their children. I must say, we did a great job raising our daughter and son.

Chapter 8

In 2003, our fourth grandbaby was born. We call him Poppa. That time my daughter was in labor for three days, and my sister and I were there with her. My husband and son took care of our daughter's other three children, working in shifts, while I was at the hospital with her. On the second day they wanted Mommy and Grandma, so I went home and my sister stayed with my daughter. I don't believe in letting children sleep in their parents' bed, and our own children never slept with me and my husband when they were little. But I was so exhausted that night that my grandbabies fell asleep with me. When I awoke the next morning, for a moment I thought that I was paralyzed again. Actually I just had two sleeping grandchildren on top of me, one lying on my hip and the other lying across my head. We must have slept that way all night, because the left side of my body and one side of my face were numb. I guess you can call that my MS scare for the year. At least I didn't need any steroids—just two children to be moved off me.

My daughter had to have a C-section, so when she came home from the hospital, I helped her out as much as I could. Besides cooking, I fed and bathed two little children. Our son offered to cancel his vacation, but we told him to go and enjoy himself. My husband took care of our grandbabies when he came home from work. It all worked out and we made it through. That time took a toll on my body, but again, rest and plenty of sleep was all I needed to feel 100 percent again.

In August 2004, my dad got a diagnosis of prostate cancer. My parents had five girls and no boys, so we all were Daddy's little girls. I'm the fourth child and the strongest of us. When my dad told us about his cancer, I promised him that, God willing, I would be there from the beginning to the end. My heart broke for my mom, because they had been together for more than fifty years. We all were nervous, unsure of where this new journey was going to take us.

I had to fight with my dad's HMO about when he would begin his treatments. In my opinion, HMOs have too many patients and not enough doctors, and the doctors don't have enough time to spend with their patients. My dad was put off, over and over again, by his doctor's office. Finally I took it upon myself to call his doctors and request an urgent appointment, but I was told that he had gotten his diagnosis only a month earlier and that he was not that doctor's only patient. I flipped out. I told the woman on the other end of the phone that my dad was the only father I had and that even though he might not mean anything to her, he meant the world to me. I also said a few other things that I won't mention, and my dad ended up with an appointment for the very next day.

I didn't attend that first appointment with my dad. The doctor and his staff asked my parents where I was, but I wanted to give them their privacy. My dad was seventy-four years old and working for the National Institute of Health, so they took over his care and treatments. Raising hell with his HMO had worked, but the NIH was a better option for him. He started with radiation treatments five days a week for about five months, and my mom and I were right there with him. I would leave my home in Maryland at seven o'clock every morning, drive to DC, pick up my parents, and drive them to Bethesda for his treatments. Afterward I'd drive back to their home, stay for a little while, and head for home around six thirty or seven in the evening. Once I got home, I got myself ready for the next day and asked God to give me the strength that I needed to make it through this trial.

My dad took steroids by mouth as part of his treatment, so he and I would talk about the never-ending hunger and the moon face he was starting to get from the side effects. My husband, sisters, and brothers-in-law would come to some of his treatments when they could, but everyone worked except me. God works in mysterious ways. I was the only one of the girls not working, and the one who could really deal with what was going on with our dad.

After his radiation treatments ended, he had to start chemo. The only side effects from his chemo treatments were hair loss and fatigue, which was another symptom he and I could discuss. My dad was the only person I knew who could eat while the chemo was actually dripping into his veins. My mom, dad, and I would stop at KFC on the way home from his chemo treatments because he would still be hungry.

During his treatment, he had a perforated colon, which needed to be operated on ASAP. His surgery was late one evening, around ten thirty, and the whole family was there. We stayed at the hospital until three thirty the next morning, because we all needed to see our dad before we went home. Even after his surgery, he had a smile on his face. He was being strong for his wife and daughters. He wore a colostomy bag for about five months. When they removed the bag and repaired his colon, we received the news that the cancer had spread to his liver and bones.

I had dealt with my mother-in-law and brother-in-law, both of whom had died from cancer, so I knew this was not good news. We traveled back and forth for about two weeks to visit our dad in the hospital. Even after the radiation and chemo treatments, cancer was taking over his body. He was hospitalized several times, but he never complained. When we asked him how he felt, he would say, "Just fine. I'm okay." One day he asked me to walk the hospital hallway with him, and we walked in silence. No words needed to be spoken, because we knew. I missed only two treatments in the two years that my dad was sick. I was worn out mentally, but I missed those two appointments because I was also worn out physically.

As time passed, things got worse. He wasn't able to hold down food, so he wasn't eating much. As the pain got worse, he started talking less and less. One Friday morning, my mom phoned and asked my husband and me to pick up my dad and take him back to the hospital. He was having a hard time breathing, even though he had just been released from the hospital on the previous day. As my husband and I hurried to get dressed, I told him that I was moving in with my mom that day to help her take care of my dad. My husband had lost his mom and brother to cancer, so he understood what I was going through. When we got to my parents' home, I told them that I was moving in with them whether they liked it or not. They both just smiled.

My mom and I slept—or just rested, more often—two or three hours a night. On Sunday, when my husband got off work, he moved in with us. My husband gives me my MS shot on Sunday nights, so that I can sleep off any side effects. Before he moved in with us, my mom and I were up most of the night. That Sunday night, however, we all three slept all night—me, Mom, and Dad. I think my dad felt safe, knowing that my mom and I weren't alone with him. As sick as he was, he was still trying to be independent.

By that time the cancer had spread to his spine. To get back and forth to the bathroom, he used a cane plus my husband and me on either side of him. My baby sister had brought some movies over for him to watch, but I think by that time he had lost most of his sight. He said that he wanted to see *King Kong*—the version with Jessica Lange—so my husband put the DVD in for him. They sat and watched it together while my mom went to eat and I went to bathe. Our dad was never left by himself—someone was always there with him. The movie was so loud that I could hear it while I was in the shower. After I got dressed, I sat and watched the movie with him. Finally he said, "Gwenie, this sure is a long movie." I asked him if he wanted me to turn it off, and he nodded yes. Then my husband and I helped him to the bathroom. My dad rubbed my hand as we were walking to the bathroom, as if to tell me that everything was going to be all right and he wanted to thank me for being here. I still cry every time I think of that. I'm crying now. After we got him back to their bedroom, he hung his eyeglasses from his T-shirt and went to sleep.

Sometime during the early morning of May 30, 2006, our dad passed away. It was a peaceful passing. We did not know he was gone until my mom tried to wake him up that morning. I believe that he passed away around 2:40 a.m., because when I went downstairs to get the phone book so that I could start calling family members and friends, something told me to look at the clock. The kitchen clock was stuck on 2:40 a.m., and the second hand was just clicking as if it was trying to move. I felt like that was our daddy's way of letting us know what time he left us. We let the clock stay like that so the rest of the family could see it. Later that day, my son changed the batteries and set the time on that clock.

Our dad saw heaven the day before he passed. I say this because my sister Carole was in the room with him when he got up out of his recliner on his own, went to the window, and raised the blinds. She said that he kept saying, "Oh wow, oh wow," while looking from side to side in amazement. Then he walked back to his chair, sat down, and fell asleep. I had seen him, in those last few days, trying to get out of his chair, as if someone was calling him or he had somewhere to go. He did have somewhere to go—home to God. God allowed me to keep my promise to my dad. I was there from the beginning to the end, just as I had promised him. God also answered our prayers about not letting our dad suffer. From what we saw in his last days, he didn't.

In the cycle of life, God takes a life and gives us a brand new life. A few days after my dad passed, our daughter told us that she was pregnant. Such deep pain and sorrow was followed eight months later by the birth of our fifth grandbaby. I stayed with our mom for the next couple of weeks.

During the two years I helped to take care of our dad, I didn't have a major attack. I had little symptoms like hot, cold, and numb feet, weakness, tingling in my hands and feet, and dizzy spells. But in August 2006, three months after our dad passed, I had a major attack. I had so much pain in my spine that it hurt to stand, walk, lie down, or even sit up. That time I called my neurologist right away. She told me that she had wondered whether something might happen, because of the stress that I had experienced while taking care of my dad. She ordered my IV steroid treatments and I recovered quickly, in about three weeks.

The strange thing was that I had no side effects from that course of steroid treatments. No moon face, no bad temper … I even got a few nights' sleep. That time, my dad was watching over me. Thanks, Daddy. One night I dreamed that my dad and I were going up the stairs to a huge mansion with large pillars on each side. Just as he was about to go through the doorway, and I was on the last step before I was to enter, he turned to me and said, "Gwenie, I really like it here." Then he disappeared and I woke up. My dad was letting me know that he was okay.

In Loving Memory of
Morrison F. Thomas
Sunrise - February 14, 1931
Sunset - May 30, 2006

Monday, June 5, 2006

Visitation - 10:00 A.M.
Mass of Christian Burial - 11:00 A.M.
St. Francis de Sales Catholic Church
2015 Rhode Island Avenue, N.E.
Washington, D.C.

Rev. Carl Dianda, Pastor/Celebrant
Mr. Rivers McCreary, Musician

My Dad

Chapter 9

Our fifth and last grandbaby (so far) was born in January 2007. She's a girl, and we call her Punky. My husband and I traveled to Jamaica to visit my daughter's family and meet Punky in March. I used to be able to fly without any problems, but on that flight I got extremely dizzy when we reached cruising altitude. With the dizziness came a feeling of insufficient oxygen, but I just closed my eyes and rode it out. We arrived in Jamaica in about three hours. I held my new grandbaby from the time I arrived in Jamaica until my visit ended.

I miss my daughter, son-in-law, and four grandbabies who live in Jamaica. Our daughter tries to come home when the kids are on Christmas break or during the summer, and I try to visit them two or three times a year. My husband can't always travel with me because of his job, so in December 2007, I decided to travel alone to Jamaica. I had not seen my family in Jamaica since Punky was born, and she would be turning one year old in January.

Thank God, the plane was half empty, so I had the whole row to myself. Back then the airlines were still serving breakfast. I ate my bacon, eggs, and muffin, and then I tried to open what I thought was juice. My hand strength varies wildly, and when I pulled the lid halfway back, it splashed on my face and clothes. It turned out that my "juice" was actually vanilla yogurt. I pulled my mirror out of my pocketbook and saw little white dots all over my face. Of course I started laughing uncontrollably as I wiped my face with a napkin. Good thing I was listening to my iPod, because some of the flight attendants and passengers started laughing too. They either assumed that what I was listening to was funny, or they were laughing at me covered in white dots of yogurt. I chose to believe that they thought I was listening to something funny. My mother-in-law used to call me Lucy, as in Lucille Ball, and now I know why.

I stayed in Jamaica for two weeks. On my flight home, the dizziness started again. I wanted to grab the woman sitting next to me and tell her that I was going to pass out, but things were already bad enough with her. As I had tried to cut my chicken, a couple of tines had snapped off my plastic fork and hit the woman and her traveling companion. So I calmed myself down, despite my dizziness, and told myself that I would be all right. I didn't want them to think that I was nuts—throwing pieces of my fork at them, and then grabbing her and screaming. Needless to say, I don't fly alone anymore.

In 2008, my mom became ill. She was so run-down that she caught what we thought was a bad cold. She was eating very little and starting to lose weight. We also assumed that she was depressed because of the loss of her husband, our dad. So I started going back and forth with her to the doctors, sometimes two to three days a week. The doctors finally discovered that she had fluid on her lungs, which needed to be drained ASAP. There I went again, struggling with her HMO. They told us about her lungs on a Thursday, but they said she couldn't be seen by a specialist until late the following week at the earliest. Suffice it to say that I had my mom in the specialist's office the very next morning.

My Mom

After the fluid was drained off her lungs, my mom was told that she needed a lung biopsy. Of course, one of my first thoughts was that word that I hate so much—*cancer*. After the biopsy, however, the test results showed no cancer, but she had to be treated for a year with antibiotics. So for the next year, I routinely drove from my home in Maryland to my mom's house in DC, and then to her doctor's office back in Maryland. On Saturdays I went over to my mom's house to change the sheets on her bed. When you're sick and you have to spend time in bed, something about the smell of clean sheets makes you feel just a little better. The good news is that after her one-year course of antibiotics, my mom is doing well. On the day of her last appointment, we celebrated with a nice lunch. Then we did some shopping and just walked around outside the mall. I missed only one of my mom's appointments, when I went to Jamaica to see my grandbabies. We all made it though another trial. God is good.

Our daughter let us know in June 2009 that she and our grandchildren would be coming home to visit us from July 8 to August 4. I could hardly wait to see them all, so I started counting down the days. It had been five months since I had last seen them in Jamaica. Since our son and his daughter had moved out, my husband and I had been alone in our house, enjoying peace and quiet, available bathrooms, and no tripping over little ones.

By the evening of July 8, however, we were surrounded by little ones crying, running around the house, and slamming doors. Little voices kept saying, "I have to use the bathroom. Who's in there?" Simply replying "Use the bathroom upstairs" did no good. If we didn't tell them where to go, they would just keep repeating, "Who's in there?"

Our two-person household turned into an eight-person household overnight. Sweetie Girl, our oldest grandbaby, also stayed with us the whole time her cousins and auntie were here, and her dad came over every day after work and on the weekends. I would get up at six o'clock to shower and get out of the way before the troops awoke. We went from one trash bag twice a week to daily trash bags full of paper cups, paper bowls, plastic forks, and plastic spoons. (No plastic knives, since the house was filled with children ranging in age from two to ten.) Thank God for dishwashers.

My family is such a blessing to me, and it was great having all of us together. The hugs, kisses, and laughter turned "I don't feel good today" into "Life is good." We went shopping, cooked out, and went swimming. I even taught three of my grandbabies how to swim. My husband helped feed the children in the mornings before he went to work. They also kept my kitchen clean. They love pizza, so we ordered pizza a lot. I even jumped rope with my grandbabies and my two big babies. I was about to turn fifty-one years old that September, and I outjumped them all. We had a speed jumping contest, which meant that the faster they turned, the faster you had to jump. I was the winner. Grandma still has it. I'm number one.

When my children took their children out for sightseeing or ice cream, I would close the door behind them and tell my husband to just listen. The silence was so nice, for the short time they were gone, that I would fall asleep. We have a three-bedroom, three-story house, and all nine of us would gather in our bedroom. I've noticed that MS has changed things in my life over the years, but it hasn't changed me. Crowds are now too much for me, with people going in all different directions. Loud voices and too much noise bother me, and I don't have the patience that I used to have. I realize that some of these changes have more to do with age. And yet, even with the noise, crying, and running around the house, I wouldn't have changed a thing. I would do it all over again, except that I would take a few days' vacation for myself during their visit. A couple of nights in a hotel would do just fine.

Here we are in a family portrait that was taken at the end of July 2009, while we were all together. The ages range from Granddaddy, who's fifty-two years old, to Punky, who is just two.

On August 4, our daughter and four of our five grandbabies returned home to Jamaica. Our daughter used to tell us not to kiss or hug her at the airport, because she would start crying. So we'd just say goodbye and remind her to call us when she got home. Of course, we always kissed and hugged our grandbabies. Abbey, our grandson, always cries when he has to say goodbye. I usually can hold back my tears until I get home and it hits me that I won't see them again for at least six months. But when Abbey fell into his granddaddy's arms and started to cry, the tears rolled down my face. Our daughter had stopped crying, because she had to gather her four children and keep track of them before her flight left. She said, "Look, Mommy is crying," and called me a big baby. It always breaks my heart to see them walking away from me.

It is now August 2017. My last MS attack and steroid treatments were one year ago. My body and mind have been fighting MS for the last twenty-three years. So far, however, I seem to be winning the battle. I will continue to fight this disease, giving it my all until someone finds a cure. Like my husband had printed on the back of one of our MS walk T-shirts, "I'm striking a blow against what I call my little monster, MS."

Live, love, and laugh.

Dedicated to Grandma

From Dee,

She has sunken to the bottom of her dark abyss,
away from the comforts this world can offer,
she knows what it is to be depressed,
to be in a room full of people and feel alone,
lost in the thoughts of her repulsive reality,
he visits her everyday;
her thoughts,
with his grotesque face,
reminding her of how "messed up" she is,
little does she know, that all this will come to past,
ephemeral; is her pain,
that her nadir will result in her zenith,
that the tragedies which befall her now, she will learn to appreciate,
for those trials will mold her into the beautiful soul she will become,
she will be
loved because of it,
she will be grateful,
for how can you appreciate health if you have not endured sickness?
how can you appreciate tranquility if you have not been in a
pandemonium?
how can you appreciate solace if you have not experienced pain?
rocky roads lead to beautiful destinations
there is beauty in hardships if they are endured with patience,
true beauty is attained through bloodshed.

-inkofdeda

Author Biography

Let me introduce myself. My name is Gwendolyn Powell, but my family and friends call me Gwenie. I was born in Washington, DC, on September 14, 1958. I am the fourth of five girls. I live in Maryland with the love of my life, my husband, Timothy. We have been married for forty years. I am the mother of two children and the grandmother of six.

My parents instilled in me the importance of faith, family, and friends. They taught me that no matter what I might be going through, someone else's challenges and difficulties are greater than mine. Those words helped prepare me for a diagnosis of multiple sclerosis in 1994. Since then, I have experienced paralysis, blindness, numbness from my neck down, and double vision, along with many other MS symptoms. I could have given up a long time ago, but instead I chose to fight—and my family has been right there with me. Don't get me wrong. I've been knocked down by MS many times, but always, after I regain enough strength, I choose to get right back up. Rather than crying "Why *me?*" I prefer to ask "Why *not* me?"

Four members of my family have multiple sclerosis, or what I call "my little monster." I was the first one to get a diagnosis, so I was able to help ease some of the fears and concerns of the others. I have laughed and cried with them, prayed and wept for them, and sat beside them in silence when no words of comfort were enough. I've cooked for them and fed them when they were too weak to feed themselves. I was there when my niece took her first breath, and when my brother-in-law took his last.

I wrote this book not only for those of you dealing with MS, but for anyone facing a challenge that you feel you might not be able to handle. I know you've heard it said many times, but you are *not* alone. Always keep your illness behind you. Never let it define who you are. I'm not saying to ignore what you're going through, but keep it on its toes. Stand tall, stand straight, and fight. Some people might abandon you when you need them the most, but new friends and relationships will enter your life. Keep smiling and laughing. Enjoy this new chapter in your life. Love is a powerful thing.

Credits to Timothy J. Powell, Timothy J. Powell 11, and Niani T. Powell for the Front and Back Cover pictures.
and
Credits to Allison Fax for the Make Up.

Printed in the United States
By Bookmasters